Mobile Homes

Graham Rickard

Lerner Publications Company
Minneapolis

All words printed in **bold** are explained
in the glossary on page 30.

Cover Illustration *A group of nomadic people outside
their mobile home in Afghanistan*

First published in the U.S. in 1989 by Lerner Publications
Company.

Copyright © 1988 Wayland (Publishers) Ltd.,
Hove, East Sussex. First published in 1988 by Wayland
(Publishers) Ltd.

Library of Congress Cataloging-in-Publication Data

Rickard, Graham.
    Mobile homes.

    Summary: Describes life in a variety of mobile homes,
including circus caravans, tents, trailers, and houseboats.
    1. Mobile home living—Juvenile literature. 2. Mobile
homes—Juvenile literature. [1. Mobile homes. 2. Mobile
home living] I. Title.
TX1106.R53   1989   643'.2   88-23108
ISBN 0-8225-2130-X (lib. bdg.)

Printed in Italy by G. Canale & C.S.p.A., Turin
Bound in the United States of America

1   2   3   4   5   6   7   8   9   10   97   96   95   94   93   92   91   90   89

Contents

Homes on the move

Everyone needs a home. To survive, humans need air, food, water, and some form of shelter to protect their families and possessions. As well as providing shelter, homes are places where families can eat, sleep, and relax with their friends in safety and comfort. Throughout the world, people live in many different types of homes, depending on the local climate and the building materials that are available.

Most people live in solid, permanent homes, which are firmly fixed to the ground. They do not have to travel far when they leave their homes to go to work, to gather food, or to tend their animals. But in many parts of the world, there are people called **nomads**, who have no fixed homes.

Above   *An Indian traveling family from Rajasthan load up the donkey as they prepare to move on.*

Right   *These nomads live in a circular tent called a yurt.*

4

Nomads spend their lives traveling long distances in search of work, water, and fresh **pastures** for their animals.

Nomads sometimes build temporary shelters, such as the snow **igloos** the **Inuit** construct as they follow herds of wild reindeer on winter hunting trips. But most traveling people live in some kind of mobile home which they can pack up and take with them when it is time to move on.

There are three main types of mobile homes—tents, homes on wheels, and boats. People live in the type of mobile home that suits their work and the climate and countryside in which they live.

Left A large modern mobile home in Arizona

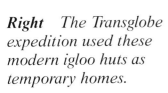

Right The Transglobe expedition used these modern igloo huts as temporary homes.

The history of mobile homes

The world's earliest people were nomadic hunters, who were continually on the move in search of food. They followed **migrating** herds of wild animals and gathered nuts, fruit, seeds, and roots. The early nomads lived in caves and simple shelters, using whatever materials were available to build their homes. They used rocks, grass, tree branches, and animal skins. When they moved on, they took the most important parts of their shelters with them, to be reused when they next found a place to stay. When people later learned how to raise animals and plants, they no longer had to travel such long distances in search of food. They settled down in stronger and more permanent homes.

However, some people have never given up their nomadic way of life, and have kept their distinctive traditional **cultures** to the present day. These peoples include the Bedouin tribes, who live in the desert and have to move around to find enough water and food for their flocks of sheep and goats. Gypsies have always had to live on the move, in search of work and markets for their goods.

Mobile homes play an important

Right   Scientists believe that nomadic Ice Age families used caves as shelter from the weather and from wild animals. Such families lived on game caught in the surrounding area, and they clothed themselves with dried animal skins. When the animals migrated, so did the humans.

part in times of war, and some of the world's great armies have lived in vast camps of tents and wagons as they marched to battle. Modern armies still use many different types of mobile homes, not only for living quarters, but also as offices and hospitals.

In the nineteenth century, thousands of European settlers moved across North America and southern Africa in search of a new life for themselves and their families. These settlers lived in covered wagons as they founded new countries that were to become very powerful.

In the modern world, many nomads are giving up their traveling way of life and settling down in permanent homes.

Above Medieval armies lived in brightly colored circular tents.

Below Early American settlers traveled together in wagon trains.

Gypsy caravans

The Gypsy people (also known as the Romany) are a nomadic people. The word gypsy is a shortened form of the word "Egyptian," although this ethnic group originally came from northern India. Gypsies began their nomadic way of life about a thousand years ago, by traveling through Africa, Europe, and Asia.

The Gypsy people are now found on almost every continent. They earn a living by selling homemade goods, and by doing seasonal work, such as picking fruit. They speak their own Romany language, and they have a rich traditional culture that includes Spanish **flamenco** music. They meet at annual Romany fairs to sell horses, tell stories, and play their music. In many European countries, such as Hungary, Gypsy musicians entertain restaurant customers by playing at their tables.

The earliest Gypsy people lived in tents, as they traveled from town to town. They began to travel in wagons when they started to raise and sell horses. Traditional Gypsy wagons were made of wood, had a rounded roof, and were pulled by horses. Every outside surface was brightly painted with colorful designs. The wagons ran on wooden wheels bound with metal hoops before rubber tires were invented.

A large family often lived together

Right   This modern Gypsy caravan is spacious and comfortable. It has been furnished in the traditional style, with leaded windows, varnished wood, and gas lamps.

for water, electricity, and television. The children usually go to local schools.

In Ireland, it is still possible to hire a traditional horse-drawn Gypsy wagon for a relaxing tour along the country lanes from one village to the next.

Left   This Gypsy woman, who tells fortunes at fairs, lives in a traditional caravan.

Below   A French Romany, who plays flamenco music on the guitar

in one wagon, so there was very little space to spare inside. A wood-burning stove was used for all heating and cooking, and the lighting came from candles and oil lamps. Gypsy wagons may have been very cramped, but they were also very attractive. They were decorated with brass fittings and had richly colored furnishings.

Many Gypsies have now given up their nomadic life, and live in large trailer homes on special sites. These modern trailers have utility hookups

9

Covered wagons

In the nineteenth century, the continents of North and South America, Africa, and Australia were opened up by European settlers. Entire families gave up their homes and jobs in Europe to sail the seas in search of a new life and a piece of land to call their own.

Encouraged by the United States government, millions of immigrants poured into North America. While the eastern half of the New World was quickly populated, the rest of the continent—with its rich pastures and other natural resources—was slow to be claimed by settlers. The new settlers used wooden wagons, covered with canvas stretched over wooden or metal hoops. These simple horse-drawn wagons carried all the supplies and possessions of the pioneer families. Each family lived in its wagon as it made its way westward across the continent. Cowboys who were taking their cattle to market on a long journey called a "cattle drive" used similar wagons to haul their food and water.

The wagons were crowded and uncomfortable. The travelers always had to make sure that they had enough food, water, and firewood. The settlers traveled in large groups called "wagon trains" for protection. The wagon train acted as a defense against hostile North American Indian tribes, bandits, and wild animals. It was the covered wagon that made the opening of the "Wild West"—and the growth of the modern United States—possible.

Many other Europeans settled in the southern tip of Africa. When Britain took control of the area in the early 1800s, thousands of Dutch

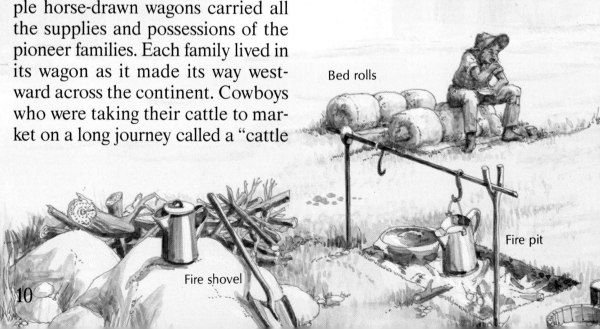

Bed rolls

Fire pit

Fire shovel

settlers (called Afrikaners) decided to leave in search of new lands. Like settlers in the United States, pioneers in southern Africa used wagons to carry their families and to protect themselves against the native African peoples whose land they were claiming. The "Great Trek" lasted from the mid-1830s to the mid-1840s, as these "Voortrekkers" traveled north to escape from British rule. The families lived and slept in their wagons until they found new lands to farm, and they carried everything they needed with them. When they finally settled down, the Voortrekkers laid the foundations of the country that we know now as South Africa.

Chuck wagon

Water barrel

Dutch oven

American cattle drivers carried their food, water, and cooking utensils in a chuck wagon. Once the cattle were settled down for the night, the cowboys would open the wagon and cook their food on an open fire.

Fairs and circuses

Fairs have been held throughout both America and Europe for hundreds of years. At first, these regular occasions were used by farmers and merchants to sell their goods. Soon fairs began to attract wandering bands of musicians and magicians. Entertainers, such as fire-eaters, puppeteers, and animal trainers, eventually took over the trade fairs. Traveling fairs and circuses became very popular in the nineteenth century, when the Barnum & Bailey's Circus toured the world. Known as "The Greatest Show on Earth," it gave several spectacular performances a day.

As they traveled from town to town with their shows, circus and fairground families lived in small horse-drawn wagons, similar to the ones used by Gypsies. But in the 1880s, they started to use large steam engines to provide power and electricity for their shows, and to pull their wagons. These steam engines were much more powerful than horses, and performers' wagons became much bigger. They were made of wood, could be over 6 feet wide, almost 13 feet high, and 20 to 30 feet long, and could weigh as much

Above *A brightly decorated steam engine, used to pull fairground rides and the showperson's wagon*

Right *Modern circus trailers in Australia*

as 7 tons. Inside, they were divided into small rooms, and children often had their own tiny bedrooms. The wagons had no toilets or bathrooms, and all water had to be carried in special covered buckets. Oil lamps were used for lighting, and the cast-iron kitchen stove was used for cooking and heating. The stove was often fitted with a brass rail, and all the shelves had a wooden lip, to stop pots and pans and other objects from falling when the wagon was on the move.

The showpeople were very proud of their wagons, which were painted with bright designs and decorated with gold leaf, brass fittings, and mirrors. The wagons were very comfortable, and the fairground families were happy to live in them all year long. Gasoline and diesel engines have replaced those powered by steam, and the wagon bodies are often made of aluminum instead of wood. The lighter aluminum wagons are fitted with more modern facilities. Today's wagons often have gas stoves and battery-powered televisions.

Traditional tents

Many nomadic people throughout the world choose to live in tents, which are light and fairly easy to put up and take down. There are many different types of tents. Nomads use the type of tent that suits their local climate and the available materials. Most tents consist of a waterproof covering supported by some kind of framework.

Native North Americans often lived in **tepees**. These are large funnel-shaped tents, made of decorated buffalo skins or tree bark on a framework of wooden poles. The poles were tied together at the top. An open fire in the center of the floor was used for cooking and heating, and smoke escaped through a hole in the roof. Tepees had a low door with a covering flap to keep out drafts. When the tribes moved on in search of new hunting grounds, the two largest tent poles were used to make a horse-drawn **travois** to carry the dismantled tepee. Many of the Inuit and **Lapp** tribes spend their summer in similar tents made of caribou or reindeer skins.

The Turkoman people live in the Iranian desert, in circular dome-topped shelters called **yurts**. The

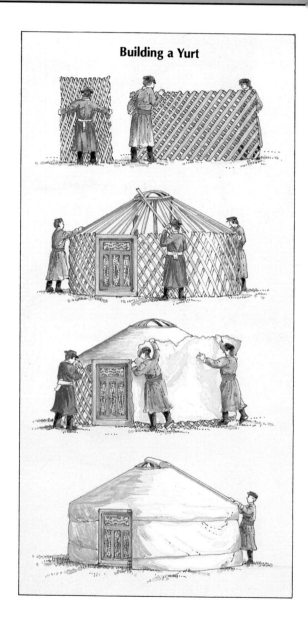

Building a Yurt

Above   A yurt is made by covering a wooden lattice framework with layers of felt.

14

Turkoman build a yurt by laying several coverings of felt over a **lattice** framework. They make their own felt by combing and pressing sheep's wool until it mats together into a flat sheet. The felt is then stretched into position over the framework. Yurts are mobile homes that can be taken apart and carried on the back of a camel, and then reassembled in half an hour.

The Bedouin tribes live in the baking heat of the Arabian desert. Bedouin tents have nine wooden poles, held up by **guy lines** attached to stakes in the sand. The poles support a cloth covering, which is made of long strips of material woven from sheep or goats' wool. The side walls can be removed to let in more air during the hottest times of the day. The inside of the tent is divided into sections for different activities, such as sleeping and eating. Bedouin tents are furnished with plenty of beautiful carpets and cushions to sit on. When the Bedouin need to find water, or fresh grazing land for their animals, they pack up their tents and load them onto their camels.

Below *These Tunisian nomads have pitched their tents in the desert.*

Modern tents

Modern tent coverings can be made of thin nylon or another **synthetic** fabric, as an alternative to the traditional felt or canvas tents. Plastic windows, mosquito netting, zippers, and sewn-in groundcloths provide extra comfort in modern tents. Wooden poles have been replaced by poles of lightweight metal **alloys** and carbon fiber. These new materials are strong, light, and versatile. Tents now come in all shapes and sizes.

Some dome-shaped tents have no poles at all. These **pneumatic** tents are held up by the air pressure in their hollow "ribs," which are inflated with a pump. Other modern tents are suspended from external poles, to give more room inside. **A-frame** tents come in many different sizes.

A long ridgepole, and a series of guy lines attached to stakes in the ground, hold the tents upright. Mountaineers and explorers often use small cylindrical tents, which are held in shape by thin rods of carbon fiber. Soldiers and hikers sometimes carry tiny one-person tents as shelter from the worst of the weather. A-frame tents often have a separate outer rain fly for extra protection. Large frame tents for family vacations have a complicated skeleton of metal poles, and have separate bedrooms inside. Today, tent camping can be very comfortable, with shower tents, chemical toilets, and bottled gas for stoves, lights, and refrigerators.

The largest tents of all are called **marquees**, and these can hold hundreds of people at social events, such as festivals and wedding receptions.

Left A modern frame tent which folds out from a trailer to provide a spacious vacation home for an entire family

Right   This modern "igloo" tent is suspended from a framework of light-weight poles.

Below   Mountaineers use tents that are small, strong, and light enough to be carried easily.

Large circular or square-shaped tents, held up by one central pole, can house many people. These tents have been used by armies for centuries. As well as housing soldiers, tents can be used in times of war as mobile offices and as hospitals. Whenever people are left homeless by disasters, such as earthquakes, floods, or wars, tents provide a quick and fairly cheap way of providing shelter for large numbers of people. They can be temporary or permanent homes.

17

Trailers and motor homes

Trailers are homes on wheels, which can be towed behind a car or truck. Similar mobile homes, called motor homes, have the driver's cab at the front and living accommodations at the rear.

Trailers and motor homes (sometimes called recreational vehicles) come in all shapes and sizes, and some are very luxurious.

Trailers are more comfortable than tents, and they are very popular as vacation homes in the U.S.A. and Europe. Many modern trailers rarely move from their permanent sites at popular vacation spots. They are rented to families throughout the vacation season. Some people live in large trailers all year, on sites that have their own stores, laundromats, electricity, and water.

Trailers vary in size from small pop-up campers, which unfold into large tentlike shelters, to enormous homes, which have to be towed by powerful trucks. Smaller trailers are cleverly designed to make the most of any available space, with tables that fold back against the wall and seats that convert into bunks. Motor homes often have an extendable roof that can be raised to provide more headroom. Modern trailers are usually very comfortable and well equipped.

Enormous motor homes, such as

Left *A modern trailer site for vacationers in West Germany. Such sites, like many in the U.S.A., have stores, showers, and other attractions for campers.*

Right *A group of young people enjoy the freedom of a vacation in a small camper van.*

Winnebagos, provide luxury living on the road. They often have several rooms, with comfortable beds and furniture, and every modern convenience. These luxury vehicles are often used by rock stars on long concert tours, or by politicians as they travel the country during election campaigns.

Some people make their own motor homes by converting old buses, ambulances, or vans into traveling homes.

Above *Large trailers are very popular for touring in Canada.*

Living on canals

In the eighteenth and nineteenth centuries, thousands of miles of **canals** were built to carry goods to the new factories and towns that were developing all over Europe and the United States. Fleets of canal boats, towed by horses, carried every kind of cargo along the new waterways. Until railways and modern roads provided a quicker method, canals were a vital means of transportation.

Canal boatmen worked long, hard hours for little wages. They could not afford to buy their own houses, so they lived with their families in tiny cabins at the rear of their boats. These canal boat families were sometimes known as "water gypsies."

They formed a close community with its own way of life and traditions. The whole family helped the boatman with his work. His wife often took turns steering, while the children led the horse along the **towpath** and helped their father with the **lock** gates, which they had to open several times a day.

Living conditions on board a canal boat were very cramped, and privacy was impossible. But the canal people were very proud of their boats, which were brightly painted inside and out. Inside the cabin, the coal-burning kitchen stove was the center of family life, and the only source of heat. To save space, cupboard doors folded down to make a table, and beds were

Right *The cabin of this traditional canal boat once housed an entire family. The kitchen stove, brass ornaments, and hand-painted decorations are very typical of this sort of boat.*

Left   Two canal boats in a lock wait for the gates to open.

Below   Breakfast time on the canal for a family vacationing aboard a spacious remodeled canal boat

used as seats during the day. Decorative plates and brass ornaments were displayed on the walls of the cabin. Families passed the time making ornamental braids and knots to decorate the outside of the boat, and furnishings for the inside.

Traditional canal life has now disappeared, but thousands of people can still enjoy the peace and freedom of the waterways. They live for a few weeks on old canal boats that have been converted into floating vacation homes.

Living on boats

Many of the world's great cities have rivers and canals flowing through them. In Venice, for example, canals are used as "streets," with boats taking the place of cars and buses as the main form of transportation. As cities grow bigger, land becomes scarce and expensive, and many people in waterfront cities choose to live on the water, in houseboats.

Amsterdam has more than a hundred canals, and many people live on colorful houseboats. The city's famous flower market, called the Singel, is a collection of floating rafts. In London, people also live in houseboats, moored on the banks of the River Thames. These homes are usually fairly large, with several rooms and comfortable furniture, and they are rarely moved from their moorings. A long **gangplank** connects them to the shore.

Hong Kong is one of the world's most crowded cities, and many families live in the harbor, on traditional boats called "sampans." The sampans are packed tightly together in rows. People may have to walk across their neighbors' boats to reach the shore.

In southeast Asia, the Bajau people live on their boats as they sail from island to island selling their catches of fish. The Bajau families live on sailing boats called "lipas." It is a cramped existence, with little protection from the weather. Some Bajau families live on larger houseboats, which have a roof of rush matting supported by bamboo poles.

In Kashmir in northern India, some people live on the lakes, in magnificent multi-storied houseboats. They use smaller boats to row to the shore and do most of their shopping from the floating shopboats that visit them.

Above *A wooden houseboat on a lake in Kashmir, northern India*

Right · *Many families live in these sampans, packed together in Hong Kong harbor.*

Below · *In the Philippines, these Bajau people live and work on the water.*

Homes on the sea

Above *Hundreds of people live on this British Royal Navy aircraft carrier.*

Many thousands of people make their living from the sea. These people often have to live on their ships for a long time. Most of the space on these ships is taken up by the engines, cargo, and equipment. The crew members usually have little room to eat, sleep, or relax. On trawlers and other small fishing vessels, the crew sleep in bunks and cook in a small **galley**. All the plates and kitchen utensils have to be carefully stored, to stop them from rolling around when the sea is rough.

Oil tankers and other large merchant ships travel on much longer journeys than do small vessels. They are often at sea for several months. These ships usually have much better facilities, with well-equipped kitchens, bathrooms, and relaxation areas for the crew. The crew members sleep in bunk beds that are quite narrow in order to save space. The crew works in shifts to operate the ship.

The navies of the world also send ships on long voyages. The ships carry thousands of people, who all need somewhere to eat, sleep, and spend their leisure time. Large naval ships, such as aircraft carriers, have

to carry vast amounts of water and supplies, and they have enormous kitchens and dining halls. The crew members sleep in bunk beds, and they have little storage space for their possessions. Each officer usually has a separate cabin. There are movie theaters and games rooms where the crew can relax when they are off-duty.

Life is very different on board the great cruise ships, which carry tourists from port to port around the world. These ships are equipped like floating luxury hotels, with facilities including restaurants and bars, discotheques, swimming pools, and **casinos**. The cabins are very spacious and beautifully furnished, with private bathrooms and air-conditioning.

Above *Cargo ships have to provide living quarters for the crew during long voyages.*

Right *The* Queen Elizabeth II *is one of the world's most luxurious cruise liners.*

Living beneath the waves

Navies have been using submarines for almost 100 years. Until recently, conditions on board these underwater ships were almost unbearably cramped and uncomfortable. Modern submarines can be very large, but the living space on board is still very limited, because so much room is taken up by the engine, weapons system, control room, and **ballast tanks**. Large submarines have a crew of about 150 people. The crew works in shifts, or "watches," of four hours at a time. They sleep in separate dormitory bunks, and the officers have small private cabins.

On long missions, modern **nuclear** submarines stay underwater for months at a time. The crew never see daylight during that period. Red lighting is used at night, so that sailors will not confuse night with day. Nuclear submarines can manufacture their own fresh air and fresh water from sea water, but they have to carry everything else that is needed on long voyages. The crew members have to learn to live together in the cramped conditions and to be considerate towards each other.

Everything is done to make the crew as comfortable as possible, and to prevent them from becoming bored. The galley serves a good variety of freshly-cooked food, and the crew can choose their meals from the menu in the dining hall. They have a wide range of films, games, and other activities to fill their free time. Crew members keep fit using exercise machines.

Smaller underwater craft, called

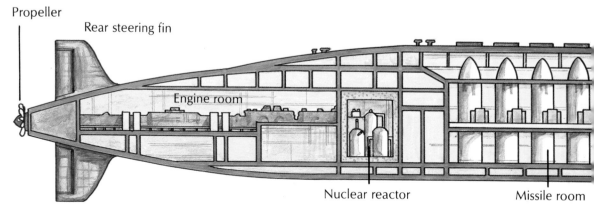

Propeller

Rear steering fin

Engine room

Nuclear reactor

Missile room

submersibles, are often used by oil companies and other businesses for inspecting and repairing oil rigs and pipelines. Submersibles have even less space for their crew than submarines, but they usually stay under water for only a short time.

Right   *A diagram showing a small submersible used by divers working beneath the waves*

Below   *Even billion-dollar nuclear submarines have little room for living space.*

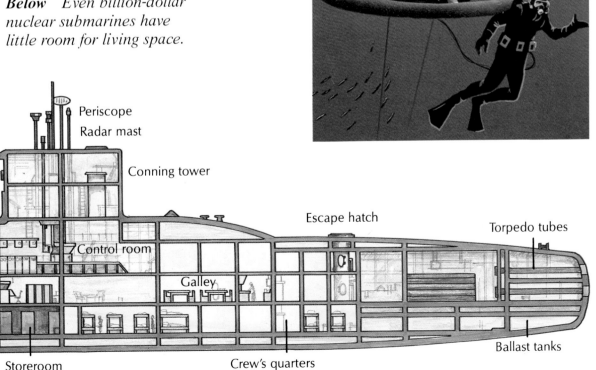

Periscope
Radar mast
Conning tower
Control room
Escape hatch
Torpedo tubes
Galley
Ballast tanks
Storeroom
Crew's quarters

Living in space

Living in space presents humans with serious problems to overcome, such as weightlessness and extremes of temperature. To survive, we need air, food, water, and warmth. Homes in space have to provide **astronauts** with all of these essentials.

The first man in space was the Soviet **cosmonaut** Yuri Gagarin, who made a complete orbit of the Earth in 1961. He and other early astronauts wore pressurized suits and traveled in tiny capsules, with no facilities or room to move around. As space flights became longer and spacecraft grew larger, conditions became more comfortable.

In 1973, *Skylab*, a large U.S. space station, was put into permanent orbit

in space. It was visited by several crews of astronauts. Most of *Skylab* was taken up by workshops and laboratories, but the living quarters were large enough for the crew to live comfortably without having to wear space suits. In 1987, a Soviet cosmonaut set a new record by staying in orbit for 238 days on the Soviet space station *Mir*.

A new era in space flight started in 1981, with the launch of *Columbia*, the world's first reusable space shuttle. The space shuttle can carry a crew of up to seven people. It is fairly spacious, with living quarters that are separate from the flight deck and cargo hold. Astronauts have a wide choice of packaged drinks and food which they can cook for themselves in the shuttle's well-equipped galley. There is no need to wear space suits or oxygen masks, because the cabin is pressurized and air-conditioned.

When it is time to sleep, the astronauts must strap themselves into

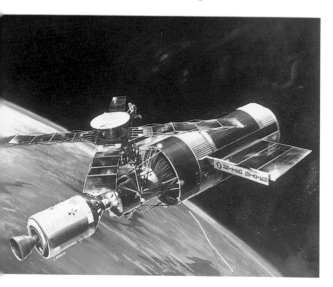

Left Skylab *was the first space station. It was roomy enough for three people to live inside comfortably.*

their sleeping bags to prevent themselves from floating around the ship.

In the future, the space shuttle will probably be used to build a large permanent space station. This station could serve as a space "port" for long missions to Mars and the other planets. Vast, spinning space cities, with **artificial gravity** and their own farms, schools, and factories, could also become a reality, if humankind decides to explore other **galaxies**.

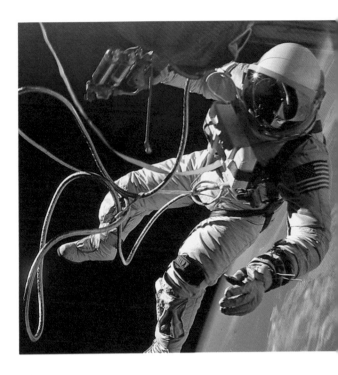

Above   *An astronaut on a space walk is protected by a space suit.*

Left   *A space colony in the future might possibly have an Earth-like landscape and artificial gravity.*

Glossary

A-frame A structure with a roof that comes to a point and stretches down to the ground; a triangular structure

alloy A mixture of two or more different metals. It has qualities different from those of its component metals.

artificial gravity An effect created in a weightless environment that causes things to have weight

astronaut Someone trained to fly in a spacecraft

ballast tanks Large hollow spaces in a submarine, which can be filled with water or air, to make the submarine sink, or rise to the surface

canal An artificial water channel

casino A public place where people gamble legally

cosmonaut A Soviet astronaut

culture The way of life shared by a group of people, including their language, arts, and beliefs

flamenco Traditional Spanish dance music

galaxy A large group of stars and planets such as the Milky Way galaxy

galley A small kitchen

gangplank A wooden plank that acts as a bridge between a boat and the shore

guy line A rope that is attached to a tent or pole at one end, and to a tent stake in the ground at the other

igloo The Inuit word for any house

Inuit A native northern people found traditionally in Greenland, Canada, Alaska, and the Aleutian Islands

Lapp A person who lives in Lapland, in northern Scandinavia

lattice A crisscross pattern of wood or bars

lock A part of a canal that can be closed off by gates. The water level can be raised or lowered to allow boats to pass from one level of water to the next.

marquee A tent used for large gatherings, such as wedding receptions

migrating Moving seasonally in search of food or warmer weather. Herds of animals and flocks of birds often migrate.

nomad A person with no permanent home, who travels searching for food, work, or pastureland

nuclear Having to do with atomic energy, which is created by controlled explosions

pasture Grazing land for animals

pneumatic Held up by air pressure

synthetic Artificial; made by human hands

tepee Traditional cone-shaped tent used by Native Americans

towpath A path running parallel to a canal, from which an animal helped tow a canal boat

travois A crude wooden platform that was used by Native Americans to haul supplies. The platform was dragged behind a horse.

yurt Traditional dome-shaped home of the Turkoman people in Iran

Books to read

Good Shelter by Judith and Bernard Rabb (New York Times Book Company, 1975)
Vans: The Personality Vehicles by Paul R. Dexler (Lerner Publications, 1977)
Shelters: From Tepee to Igloo by Harvey Weiss (Thomas Y. Crowell, 1988)
Just Look at...Living in Space by Robin Kerrod (Macdonald Educational, 1984)
Submarines by Tony Gibbons (Lerner Publications, 1987)

Houses and Homes

Building Homes
Castles and Mansions
Homes in Cold Places
Homes in Hot Places

Homes in Space
Homes in the Future
Homes on Water
Mobile Homes

Picture acknowledgements

The author and publishers would like to thank the following for allowing their illustrations to be reproduced in this book: British Waterways Board, pp. 20, 21 (both); Camera Press, p. 27 (top); Cephas Picture Library, p. 9 (top); the Hutchison Library, pp. 4 (both), 5 (top), 8; Christine Osborne, p. 15; PHOTRI, pp. 28, 29 (both); Topham Picture Library, pp. 5 (bottom), 7 (bottom), 22, 23 (bottom); Malcolm S. Walker, pp. 10-11, 14, 26-27; ZEFA Picture Library, pp. 9 (bottom), 12, 16, 17 (both), 18, 19 (both), 23 (top), 24, 25 (both); ZEFA Picture Library, *cover.* All other pictures from the Wayland Picture Library.

Index